AWAKEN THE
WIZARD WITHIN
1001

Awaken the Wizard Within 1001

Higher Self Consulting & Akashic Records Reading

MACARENA LUZ BIANCHI

Imprint

Spark Social, Inc.

Awaken the Wizard Within 1001:
Higher Self Consulting & Akashic Records Reading

ISBN: 9781736180105
Ebook: 9781736180112

Subscribe to the email list for this book spark.fyi/1001

How-to-Course Third Edition, 2020 | First Printing, 2006
Awaken the Wizard Within Level II Series

Copyright © 2020 by Macarena Luz Bianchi
macarenaluzb.com

Spark Social, Inc. Miami, FL USA sparksocialpress.com

For those who have ever felt, there is more to life than what is seen. I honor and acknowledge you for exploring that notion and having the courage to seek and discover that which is glorious and found within you.

Contents

Preparation

Your Higher Self is a Wizard!

Welcome! I hope you are as excited about your learning this material as I am. You are about to embark on a beautifully empowering experience filled with glorious wonder, wellness, and wisdom. May the information provided here give you all you need to have a smooth and fulfilling course. As your virtual Fairy Godmother, I will guide you through the process.

Read this book to align and prepare fully to access your Higher Self and the Akashic Records.

Please avoid alcohol and recreational drugs for 24 hours before playing with the Magic Key to preserve the energy field's integrity.

Wear comfortable clothes you can sweat in—some of us sweat when we are in the divine zone of pure consciousness.

Wear black socks for grounding.

Have drinking water available while you go through the material, consulting your higher self, and exploring the Akashic records.

Please have something to write to take notes with, like a journal to write in longhand unless you prefer to do so on a tablet or type faster than you write.

Join the Awaken the Wizard Within Facebook Group for Wizard Friendly & Lighthearted Metaphysical Content. Any questions that you may have about this material, you can ask in there, and soon you can ask your Higher Self/Akashic Records. You can also invite your friends with Wizard's potential. Later, you will be invited to the graduate group for Awakened Wizards.

Do you know how to muscle test yourself? Have you explored your intuitive senses? If not, check out my freebie and the Awaken the Wizard Within 101 course, Biofeedback & Muscle Testing for Muggles.

To get you in the mood, check out <u>Abraham Hicks</u> on YouTube and Akashic Records or metaphysics, etc.

Please note: You will be given the Key/Magic Key referred to throughout later in the book.

Wizarding Agreement

This is a contract between you and your higher self.

Your Wizard's preparation materials provide are to be read and practiced in their entirety; it was designed for you to be able to review its content in great depth as often as you desire. Everything on here is a prerequisite for your sacred practice.

You are within the enchanting and loving vibration of pure consciousness as you participate in an ancient process guided in a new way. Awakening the Wizard within by connecting to your higher self and communicate directly with your Akashic Records is a loving act of service to yourself and others. Your source energy will be guiding and directing your every action throughout your learning, as well as, anytime you use this tool. It is necessary to recognize that this level of work within, is your responsibility as an individual, thereby acknowledging the following agreements:

1. *I enter into this loving experience knowing that I am filled, surrounded, and protected by the love, light, and sound of pure consciousness as I understand it.*

2. *I will use what I learn with my highest integrity for the highest love of all.*

3. *With gratitude for the blessings in my life as I expand my light in this service, I take full responsibility for its use in alignment with unconditional love and Universal Law.*

4. *I will ask my higher self directly about anything within this material and the rest of the text I have not completely understood.*
   Individuals step into this work, as they are ready. It is appropriate to share information about it as long as we give the individuals the space to allow them to step up and attain it for themselves. The teaching of the Magic Key develops out of an in-depth tuning to the work. There are numerous subtle levels that are revealed over time, practice, and experience. The skills to teach are developed through an inner surrender to the energy of unconditional love and are not based on outer abilities. To assume this role without experiencing the training and mentoring necessary would not be

beneficial or provide the highest good for all. If you feel called to teach, it is important that you take the necessary training and apprentice under a teacher.

5. *I will NOT teach or pass along the Magic Key in any form to any party or persons until I have completed a full training and have been awarded approval.*

6. *For my expansion and release of limitations, when participating in the Facebook group or in any way, I give the course trainer permission to call me out and bring to my attention any limiting beliefs or disempowering language.*

7. *When practicing or working with others, the information that is revealed is private and confidential. I will respect the privacy of others and keep anything revealed confidential.*

I have read and understood this agreement and agree to the above conditions.

I continue as agreement to the above.

Sign & Date:

You can declare you signed your Wizarding Agreement on the Awaken the Wizard Within Facebook Group.

Chapter 1

Introduction

"You cannot teach people anything. You can only help them discover it within themselves." ~ Galileo

Let the Magic Begin!

Welcome to this glorious and enchanting journey! You will find it will enrich all aspects of your being with wonder, wellness, and wisdom. There is a little known secret that can awaken any mortal into a Wizard – a master of manifestation who is clever, wise, peaceful, and unreasonably happy. That secret is your higher self, a.k.a. zero-point energy, and the Akashic Records – a metaphysical field containing all thought, word, deed, and potentiality, which is available to you as your birthright. You awaken the Wizard within by connecting to your innate divinity and unlimited knowledge while actualizing your innate infinite power. Your divinity is the part of you that feels and is connected to **source**. Unlimited knowledge includes hidden and all information, which is available to you. Divinity and knowledge are necessary for balance and become wisdom when used together. Infinite power is the ability to use your gifts, master your mind, be a master of your life, and manifest at will. You are a Wizard.

This material provides the preliminary information necessary to harmonize before awakening the Wizard. Soon you will learn how to access your higher self. After completing this process, your Wizard will be fully awakened, and you will be able to consciously and directly access and experience your metaphysical nature. You will attune to the essence of this powerful vehicle of light, love, and healing while working with the precise art of asking questions and translating the information received, and you will understand the basics of consulting for others to deepen your own process. This work relies heavily on your intent and the subtle yet precise art of phrasing questions. To support your practice, you'll find examples of possible intentions and questions for your higher self throughout.

There are many ways to communicate with your higher self; here, you will learn one of them. The most direct and empowering method because it requires you to be awake, conscious, and present. I call it the Key, and it is like a charm or magic key. With it, you will communicate **consciously** and directly with source, which awakens the Wizard within. Accessing your higher self gives you access to unlimited knowledge – like having an **oracle** at your disposal. You will have *Conversations with God* like author Neale Donald Walsch whose wonderful work has let people know it is absolutely possible to have a personal and intimate relationship with the other side. Your higher self and the Akashic Records store all thought, word, and deed of all past, present, and future. Akasha or Akasa means the substance from which all life is formed, and a Record is an authentic copy of known facts.

In *The Amazing Secrets of the Masters of the Far East*, Victor Simon Perara describes:

> The Akasa is an all-**pervading**, **primordial**, **homogeneous** substance, every part or portion of which contains in potential all the powers that now and will ever exist. Every atom of the **heterogeneous** universe, being but a conditioned aspect of the homogeneous whole from which it came, contains inherent within itself all these infinite powers which are all seeking to express themselves.

In his book, *Edgar Cayce on the Akashic Records*, Kevin J. Todeschi explains:

> Akasha comes from the Sanskrit word meaning; boundless space; and is equated to the central storehouse of all information for every individual who has ever lived. More than just a reservoir of events, the Akashic Records contain every deed, word, feeling, thought, and intent

that has occurred at any time in the history of the world. Much more than simply a memory storehouse, these Akashic Records are interactive; they have tremendous influence upon our everyday lives, our relationships, our feelings and belief system, and the potentials and probabilities we draw towards us; [they] contain the history of every soul since the dawn of creation; [they] connect each of us to one another. They contain the stimulus for every archetypal symbol or mythic story which has ever deeply touched patterns of human behavior and experience. They have been the inspiration for dreams and inventions. They draw us together or repel us from one another. They mold and shape levels of human consciousness. They are a portion of Divine Mind. They are the unbiased judge and jury that attempt to guide, educate, and transform every individual to become the very best that she or he can be. They embody an ever-changing fluid array of possible futures that are called into potential as we interact and learn from the data that has already been accumulated.

So, where exactly are the **metaphysical** Akashic Records? Everywhere: within every cell of your body in your DNA, your **aura**, and in the **Akashic Dimension**. You, as well as everyone, are inherently and always connected. The Key illuminates your existing connection bringing it into consciousness while you are fully awake.

The techniques you are about to learn will give you a way to relate, interpret, and integrate the vibrational information you will receive. Read this material in order the first time so the information can build upon itself and serve as an energetic tune-up and calibration, enabling you to perceive the Wizard clearly. **Healing** and **enlightenment** occur within you every time you access the Records and when you review this material, which also deepens your experience and relationship within the Records.

I took many Akashic Records classes because they were rewarding, healing, liberating, therapeutic, and a direct experience with source and unconditionally loving. Everyone will feel a loving connection once they start **working** with their higher self.

The Records are usually referred to as a book, library, or divine light. As an extension of these **metaphors**, I use the terms "on" and "off" when speaking of using the Key to access and "in" and "out" when referring to it being activated or inactive. Though the Akashic Records are nondenominational and predate religion, this ancient magic is referred to in virtually every ancient teaching. In the Bible is known as the *Book of Life* and the Torah as the *Book of Knowledge*. Buddhism literature calls it *Nature's Memory*. In Islam, it is experienced in direct communication immediately after prayer while sitting in silence. In Christianity, Saint Peter refers to when he reviews your life at the gates of heaven. Hindu literature calls it the *Primary Principle of Nature*. Psychologist Carl

Jung called it the *Collective Unconsciousness* existing in many dimensions and timeframes. Psychologist Rupert Sheldrake describes it as *Morphic Resonance:* stating every human action and thought creates waves, like ripples on a pond, which affects all other humans. *Theta Healing, Quantum Healing,* and *Matrix Energetics* happen at this level. Theologians describe it as a universal filing system that records every thought, word, and action in the collective memory hard-drive. If it interests you, certainly explore this energy field's historical role as an exercise to practice communicating with the Key.

Accessing your higher self is subtle yet strong energy medicine. Every *time you call upon your Wizard* and *go in*, it is healing. It is not necessary to say anything while in the Records; you will receive what is necessary. You could go in and say "Harry Potter" repeatedly and get what you require; however, your thoughts and words guide source energy permitting it to assist you. Though entities come in all shades of character, nothing can do anything to you —positive or negative— light or dark magic— without your permission. Keep in mind: it does not have to be conscious permission.

Please do not worry; we have tools to release outside influences. Anytime you feel any apprehension or danger, it is wise to *connect to your Wizard* and *ask for assistance*. I use these tools regularly because we all have influences that may have already served their purpose and can be released. As a personal example, one night, my friend and I were scanning our auric fields and noticed a dark spot over my heart center. I usually do not see auras, but sometimes at night, I can see my body's energy patterns like subtle light on the outside. I have no idea how the dark spot got there or why it was there; I only knew it had to go. In a peaceful and joyous tone, I said, *"Thank you for fulfilling our agreement. It is time for you to go. I release you to the light."* I also used the *Outside Influences Charm* and the *Forgiveness Charms* (found in *More Magic for Awakened Wizards: Awaken the Wizard Within 1002*) as I moved my hands to move the energy outward from my torso. My friend, who had sight, reported that the dark spot became a large, beautiful, and translucent crystal once outside my body before it disappeared. Things are not always what they seem, and your higher self is great at illuminating these mysteries.

Chapter Glossary

For clarity, you will find definitions for the words in **bold** at the end of each chapter.

- Source: a generative force: cause, a point of origin, God or Spirit: Universe, Pure Consciousness
- Intent: your purpose or goal
- Charm: series of words used to create
- Conscious: complete perception, fully awake and fully aware

- Oracle: a person who reveals hidden knowledge or divine
- Pervading: diffused throughout every part of
- Primordial: a first created
- Homogeneous: the same, uniform structure or composition throughout
- Heterogeneous: diverse, mixed
- Metaphysical: a reality beyond what is perceptible to the senses
- Dimension: a level of existence or consciousness
- Aura: a level of existence or consciousness
- Healing: to make sound or whole
- Enlighten: to give knowledge and insight
- Work: to bring to pass; effect
- Metaphor: a symbol

Chapter 2

How to Play

Make notes and write out questions for your Higher Self as you go electronically on a device or with a quill or any writing instrument with a notebook or journal to write on.

This text is loaded with **tools**. The main one is awakening your Wizard by accessing your higher self, which has precise instructions; the rest will be scattered throughout in italics. *Try them out, use the ones you like, and adjust any of them to suit your experience.* You'll find the books I mention linked because they are powerful tools, most of which have been referred through the guidance. Tools and teachers come in all shapes and sizes; the more of them floating around in our awareness, the more options you have. Though you can access all knowledge, you/**they** will use your awareness and your experience to guide you. You will find links to all the web sites referenced throughout this material in the reference section.

Since language is **finite** and words carry many connotations, any word in bold will be defined for clarification and context. This is not a linear process, so go slowly and do not skip over any of the asides as they include vital information. Read this in order at least once, and then you may skip around as much as you like.

To create a foundation from which to work, many ideas and subjects will be covered to put us on the same page. Some of these ideas may seem extraordinary, and others may challenge the way you perceive the world. Please suspend your disbelief and disagreement to consider what is being communicated with an open mind and heart; it may help *visualize energy flowing from your heart center. If you feel tense, stop and breathe deeply to release it.* Once you access your higher self, you may *reread* this and ask for comments or clarifications. You do not have to take my word for it; you will be able to ask directly.

As you read this, be aware of what distracts you or takes you out of the flow and away from your **empowerment**. To avoid feeling uncomfortable when we're offended, triggered, embarrassed, or annoyed, we often trade **self-awareness, unconditional   love,** and **self-worth** for being comfortable. Unfortunately, we don't ask ourselves, "Is this trade worthwhile?" Is not being offended worth disconnecting? Is not being embarrassed worth shutting down? Is being annoyed worth your joy?

Is being right worth the absence of happiness? Is the fear of being challenged worth not expanding? It is amazing what our **minds** will do to retain the illusion of **control**. Please be very clear. The purpose of awakening the Wizard is SELF-AWARENESS, SELF-EMPOWERMENT, FREEDOM, and JOY – not a greater delusion of control.

Self-awareness and self-empowerment lead to **freedom** and conscious **choice** then joy. You are forming a **partnership** with pure consciousness so you may co-**create** to your full potential, the limits of which are based on how aware you choose to be and how grand you wish to play. You see, by embarking on this course, you are saying, "Thanks, mind. I do not need to be on autopilot anymore." Do you think your mind is going to say, "Finally – thank you?" Not quite. Your mind developed to keep you safe, which it defines as not changing anything. How does resistance play out for you? How does your mind keep you safe?

One day after excusing myself during a private class, I answered a phone call causing the student to feel insulted and not valued by the interruption. I apologized and agreed not to do it again. I reminded her that nothing I could do, especially taking a phone call, would diminish the gift and power of connecting with her higher self. She did not return to complete the class. When I went in to ask what happened, I discovered she felt excited and terrified because with this work comes awareness and with awareness comes full responsibility. So what happened within her? Did an **archetype** like her **Sabo-**

teur take over? Was it a timing issue in that she was not ready or willing to receive? Even though life is not linear, there is an order to events and a rhythm to our growth. Be gentle with yourself, be patient, and trust you will get through any challenging parts with ease when you're ready. For example, once upon a time during my atheist days, hearing the word God made me cringe. If I started reading and the word God appeared, I would put the material down because I did not want to hear anything about *God – the myth* I was convinced was the cause of much suffering and irrational behavior. I consequently **missed out** by applying one **assumption** about what the word meant to everyone who used it. Thanks to this work, I understand why that period of my life was necessary, and most of the challenges I experience. I also understand that everything happens for our benefit, even the *bad stuff*, which is why we refer to our challenges as playgrounds of experience.

Glossary

- Tool: a means to an end, natural ability
- They/Them: your higher metaphysical self communicating as Masters, Teachers, and Loved Ones
- Loved Ones: your physical and soul family, ancestors, and ancestral lineage

- Finite: limited, having a beginning and an end, having a limited nature of existence
- Empowerment: remembering you always have a choice; enabled, self-actualized, ability to consciously manifest
- Self-awareness: clear and constant knowledge of your physical, emotional, mental, and spiritual bodies
- Unconditional: absolute, no limits
- Love: Source energy
- Self-worth: consistently recognizing your true glory and honoring your divinity
- Mind: ego, personality, your finite self. You are not your mind; your mind is one of your tools
- Control: directing influence, to exercise restraining: usually fear-based. (As a recovering control freak, I am an expert.)
- Freedom: the ability to choose, not bound by physical, emotional, mental, or spiritual limitations
- Choice: infinite options and alternatives
- Partnership: equal
- Create: bring to existence
- Archetype: roles we play, original pattern or model, an inherited idea derived from the experience of the race, and is present in the unconscious of the individual (Carl Jung). *Sacred*

Contracts by Caroline Myss helps identify and
work with our archetypes

· Saboteur: pertaining to self-esteem, the part of
us that causes us to block our own empowerment. We all share this archetype.
· Missed out: a momentary lack of connection: it
is impossible to actually miss out on anything
· Assumption: to claim an opinion as fact, in a
world of infinite possibilities, it is not useful nor
wise to assume anything

How I Became a Wizard

"You're a wizard, Harry!" ~ Rubeus Hagrid in Harry Potter and the Sorcerer's Stone by J.K. Rowling

---

Chapter 3

BM: Before Magic

Today, I teach people to awaken the Wizard and tap into their glory through wonder, wellness, and wisdom. I get to play with empowered people who connect to unconditional love and infinite power —very loving and spiritual stuff; however, I used to be much more stubborn and an atheist —a curious muggle, but pretending to be a muggle nonetheless. I also thought my life was great and did not need anything —especially spirituality. Regardless of your background, belief system, or inner circles' opinions, higher self consulting is available to everyone, as you will recognize by my personal example.

I was born in Chile and grew up in Costa Rica and Miami. Though my parents were not religious, Costa Rica is a predominantly Catholic country. Before my sixth birthday, I remember thinking that it was time to get serious. I also contemplated that religion's problem was how people used it to displace personal responsibility —not what the other five-year-olds discussed. I was headstrong and wanted to understand everything; consequently, I drove my parents and a few nuns crazy with relentless questioning and challenges. When we moved to the States, the kids were confused since I did not fit a Spanish speaker's stereotype while I found their lack of curiosity very confusing. At twelve, my parents divorced after many miserable years together. All the while, I loved learning and being out of my unhappy house, so I enjoyed school. As it turns out, the writing was my only outlet for emotional expression.

Also significant to my development was the realization that depending on my parents was not fun. I went to work at fifteen. At sixteen, I started working at nightclubs in Miami Beach – initially at the door, then marketing, managing, and coordinating events. I lived a double life: book smart straight-A student by day and street smart door diva by night. I was interacting with a very diverse group of people, from drag queens to real royalty. I was responsible, serious, and emotionally like a brick wall. I never danced until I experimented with fun drugs —an enlightening experience that created a window on my emotional brick wall. I never drank alcohol because it wasn't yummy, and I was a bit of a control freak. I had friends who became drug addicts and others who were murdered. Thankfully my experience with drugs was illuminating and did not become a lifestyle. Though in metaphysical denial, working the door at nightclubs allowed me to finesse my intuition. I knew if people were getting in based on their *vibe*.

At nineteen, I had a heatstroke and got sick from my Coca-Cola and candy bar diet prompting me to listen to my body and read a natural healing book from *Deepak Chopra,* where I learned it was not too late to get healthy. By twenty-three, I traveled extensively, had two Bachelors of Arts, and independently owned my condo. I decided to go to graduate school for film instead of law school and graduated at twenty-five with a great job. Everything was perfect. Well, not quite... I was also emotionally shut down, and despite being thin, I was unhealthy. I joined a *gym* where the *trainer* introduced me to Yolanda Valdes, a *nutritionist*, who introduced me to Donna, a healthy *chef*, who taught me the necessity of preparing our own food because we infuse it with our personal divine energy, which seemed like a lot of mumbo jumbo to me, but I liked her food. When the ladies found out I had not had a period for over a year due to the birth control shot, they did an intervention. I thought it was great not to menstruate, so they explained about natural cycles and sent me to Dr. Janet Galipo, an *acupuncturist*, *Body Talk* practitioner, and cofounder of *BodyIntuitive*, who got my flow back. These three referred me to Jerry, a massage therapist and, little did I know, a healer, who told me I was too young to be so screwed up physically and demanded I see him once a week whether or not I could pay.

All along, I'd thought I was fine; apparently, constant tension and not sleeping were not normal. Before Magic, my life was overwhelmed with disempowerment and victim mentality and emotionally depressing, mentally confusing, and lacking in wonder.

Glossary

- Muggle: non-wizard people from the J.K. Rowling and Harry Potter universe. If you have not read these, you are missing out on fun, imagination, and adventure! Okay, now that I got that off my chest, you will not hear about it anymore. I'm done here.

Chapter 4

After Magic

April 2000 marks my Before Magic and After Magic transition when my friend Yoli introduced me to the Akashic Records, and it went something like, "This was the most AMAZING thing I have ever done —YOU HAVE TO DO IT— call her, make an appointment, NOW!" I didn't understand what the Records were, but it sounded interesting because Yoli reported that she spent the entire time talking about how two of her past lives held her back. At the time, as a habitual muggle lacking imagination, I relied only on logic and scientific data; I applied these to everything in my life —not just business and academia, where they are best suited. Fortunately, I had an issue: a dramatic and confusing break-up. I was not interested in psychics; I needed to understand destiny. I also wasn't sure about past lives, but I was curious, so I had a consultation with Lauralyn, a remarkable woman whose three-year-old son died of a brain aneurism while she was getting her Masters in Theology. Her son's passing compelled her to discover what happens when we die. Among many treasures, Lauralyn found the Records. She learned from Mary Parker, who learned from Johnny Prochaska, who was given a sacred prayer (key or charm) to consciously access the Records, which was translated from Mayan to Spanish to English a few decades ago.

I was impressed with Lauralyn because she was normal: not too angelic sounding or spacey. She was a grounded woman with normal children. No other lifetimes came up, and my consultation was very different from Yoli's. My consultation was extraordinary and a turning point in my life as it awakened the Wizard within me. I asked many questions, discussed many topics, and I was awed by the depth of it all. It made me aware I was not spiritually alone, as none of us are, even though I had lived my entire life as if it was me against the world. Since I lived my life as if I was hexed to be alone, I was very aggressive about everything —especially getting what I wanted. I believed that if I did not make anything, and everything happens, no one would. This loner syndrome was a part of my workaholism abandonment issues and the cause of my suffering.

We spent five minutes discussing my ex-boyfriend and then covered a lot of ground, based on my long list of questions. They let me know I listen in a unique frequency and, therefore, never to compare myself with anyone —sound advice for all. Like when George Lucas said it did not matter whether he went to film school or art school, he would have still made Star Wars, destiny was described as a guitar string with a specific length and infinite possibilities of sound depending on how the string is played. This is our free will. They let me know my family was not stuck though it appeared that way to me. They also said my job was appropriate at the time, and a better opportunity would eventually present itself. They told me to stop with my relentless need to save the world, which was not my burden alone since everyone plays their part. Besides, the world did not need saving; the world wants us to express ourselves truly. Energetically, it was also magical. I felt it. The consultation expanded my awareness and reconnected me to premonitions about our universal connection I barely remembered from my childhood. Essentially, they did not say much I didn't know at my core; they validated what I was afraid to admit. My shift was big and beautiful.

Six months later, while experiencing what I can only describe as energy surges in my head, I returned to Lauralyn for energy work, not knowing what that meant. I rested on Lauralyn's massage table while she placed her hands on different parts of my body. She reported that part of my aura was energetically rewired, so the energy load wouldn't freak me out and instructed her to teach me a few things because I was really concerned about managing my body with the hectic demands of filmmaking. They shared that the most important quality in food is its energy, which everyone influences and everything it comes in contact with. Naturally, any extended period of food without nutrients would break down the system like a car without fuel. This is why blessing our food is important. In the beginning, I would say, "May nothing inappropriate enter my body," which is fear-based since it implies something could hurt me. These days, I say, "I bring you into my energy field," which empowers me by acknowledging my divinity and clears whatever goes into my mouth. I was also instructed to learn and practice meditation to quiet my mind. I did not have the time, nor could I sit still, so they said five minutes was enough. First, I was to sit there. Once I was comfortable and able to be still, I could observe the thoughts, focus on the breath, and so on. They also said they wanted to work with my close associates and me, so Lauralyn was to teach us how to access our Records. What?!

It was a huge surprise to discover that anyone could communicate with this energy. There I thought Lauralyn was some genius like the Dalai Lama. We had a private class, and everyone else seemed to take to it quite easily. One friend was talking to Billie Holiday while I felt stuck and bewildered. I thought the information was coming from me since it sounded like me. I was very opinionated, and, of course, I thought I knew everything and had a robust imagination. Fortunately, I have never had a student who walked away as disillusioned as I was; I thought there was something wrong with me for not getting it like the others. When I review that first journal, it is evident I was in and communicating just fine.

The weekend after the class, I went to a Native American *Inipi* (*sweat lodge*) with Lauralyn, who drank a glass of wine. Later that night, she asked me to open my Records to read a letter she received from her ex-boyfriend's new girlfriend because she wanted to hear what her energetic team had to say about it. She could not go in herself since alcohol interrupts our energy field, allowing greater room for misinterpretation. Because I was simultaneously reading, talking, and communicating what I realized from the Records, I had no time to edit like I did while journaling in class. Information, which was way beyond my realm of knowledge or opinion, came through me, allowing me to experience the reality and accuracy of the information and realize that even I, a rationalist, could do it. By the end of the impromptu consultation, Lauralyn said I was really amazing, which I blew off like yeah, whatever.

That experience started my friendship and apprenticeship with Lauralyn and set me off running to work on myself with and through the Akashic Records. Despite the intense growth and much crying, since my emotional dam finally broke, I loved learning and was thrilled to have an appropriate teacher. As they say, "When the pupil is ready, the teacher appears," and vice versa. I loved having found a friend in Lauralyn and my invisible team of assistance because they could call me on my stuff in a loving way. Eventually, I was instructed to continue the training so that I could consult for others. While still spiritually in the closet, I attended every class I could to do my inner work and learn as much as possible. In the fall of 2000, it came forth: within twenty years, everyone would have access to the Akashic Records. I had no idea I would play a part in it. What Lauralyn learned in ten years, I learned in one year, and I pass those tools along to you. Today, Lauralyn consults with me when she wants greater objectivity. We are Akashic Records Buddies. We get together or talk over the phone with our Records open for maintenance and fun.

In the meantime, Mary Parker formed Akashic Record Consultants International, a great resource for consultants and teachers. Though honoring their work, Lauralyn eventually split from the group because she did not resonate with the organizational model into which they evolved. Many of Lauralyn's students go on to join ARC, although I did not. I've seen some of their teachers in action, and they are doing beautiful work. It's like this: I've never met a Buddhist I did not like. I love their style. I agree with everything they believe. Nevertheless, I do not wish to join their organization either.

Higher self and source consulting, a.k.a. the Akashic Records, are available to everyone. Many are already experiencing it. Guidance is given according to our belief system and what we are willing to accept. If you believe in signs, you will get signs, and if you believe spirit speaks, you will have a conversation because we create our reality. Some access it through meditation, prayer, or dreams. Some listen to guided meditations. Others invoke their guidance by simply asking, like Jesus said, "Ask, and you shall receive." Others have a consultation with a facilitator. Even better, others learn how to do it themselves consciously —like you with your new Key. Regardless of how someone connects, what is most important is the infinite, unconditionally loving, harmonizing, and healing energy of your higher self; words are limited while energy encompasses everything: mind, body, emotion, and spirit or as I like to call it glorious wonder, wellness, and wisdom.

Everything in our existence is created to evolve, such as all ideas and systems. Early on, they said I was a bridge assisting in the shift: connecting the old and new paradigm. As such, it is my duty to share this work and my experience as it evolves. The Key you are learning here is unique and was given to me to awaken and transform consciousness on a mass level as I took on the role of virtual Fairy Godmother (an endearing term my clients call me). Unlike all the others I have heard, my Key is short, to the point, and nondenominational (like me). I like that it is not based on Judeo-Christian doctrine to include and welcome everyone, regardless of any religious affiliation or agnostic background. The Key is a catalyst for you to express yourself. After Magic, my life has been enchantingly empowered, free, and joyful! The same and more await you.

Chapter 5

Sample Consultation

My First Akashic Consultation – April 2000

LB = Lauralyn, Akashic Records Facilitator
MB = Macarena

LB: Okay, your Records are open. I see a beautiful woman playing the harp. Who is this? Is this Macarena?

LB: (The Records said) No, though it represents your energy. They wish to acknowledge that you listen in the frequency of the harp.

MB: How lovely. (Confused)

LB: All right. What does that mean? (From the Records) It means you listen in a unique frequency that allows you to perceive the bigger picture.

MB: Interesting, Yes. It's what makes me a good producer.

LB: (From the Records) Yes. It is because of this listening. You do not get distracted by the noise. This is why sometimes when someone tells you their problems, you're like, "What's the problem?"

MB: Aha.

LB: (From the Records) Others do have this quality, and yet it is unique. It is like being attuned to a unique frequency giving you a unique perspective. This is one reason of many you are not to compare yourself to anyone —especially your family.

LB: Let's begin. What is your first question....

Chapter 6

Wizard Willing

"The key to growth is the introduction of higher dimensions of consciousness into our awareness." ~ *Lao Tzu*

The following are important concepts to understand before embracing your inner wizard.

Awareness is a full-time job. By awakening the Wizard within, you are **claiming** your **innate** divinity and **infinite power**. You agree to turn on all the lights so you may see, recognize, and play with **everything**. Awareness is an ongoing practice. Sometimes relationships are great awareness arenas. Like realizing what relationships are truly supposed to be: a loving environment for the individual to grow. This means we are all here to change or enjoy the amusement park ride of life —some call it growth; it is the human experience (we all do it, and no matter how connected to source we become, we are not spared the full spectrum of life). Everyone, including partners, reflects ourselves: the good, the bad, and the ugly. When I was younger, I knew If I didn't hop on this ride with one, I'd hop on another ride with some other clown/divine partner, which might have been a wild roller coaster or even a haunted house. In the end, all rides are divine, but I personally don't fancy scary ones. The best part is we get to choose our theme parks of experience, the rides, and the guests. We can all strive to be conscious in all areas of our life.

Don't think of awareness as a difficult state to acquire. Awareness is natural and readily available to us. Maintaining the filters we use to resist our inherent awareness is what is actually unpleasant or even painful. The good news is we release resistance by accepting our awareness. The great news is if we ask, our higher self will assist us in accepting what is. Accessing our higher selves reminds me of one of those old Master Card commercials:

> Internet Access: $50
> Book/Course: $299.99
> Awakening the Wizard Within: Priceless

Glossary

- Claim: to call, take rightful ownership
- Innate: originating within, existing from birth

- Infinite: limitless, endless, all-inclusive, includes you
- Power: exercising choice; authority to promote self-actualization or influence, ability to manifest or produce
- Everything: all that exists: physical and metaphysical

Chapter 7

Communicating

The following concepts are essential to consider as you communicate with your Akashic Records. Consult with your higher self should you have any questions about their relevance and how and why they may be useful to you. As you will feel, this tool is all about unconditional love and your empowerment; therefore, your higher self's perspective is very different from your human (ego) perspective. Spirit can do a lot; however, it cannot see itself, as it is not physical. We are all spiritual beings having a physical experience, not vice versa. Everyone needs to have some sort of deliberate communication with source due to the planetary changes taking place and the evolution of our metaphysical awareness.

Why are we here? What's the meaning of life? There are infinite possibilities. One answer is to express our glorious selves. Another suggests that we all were part of an experiment on separation or contrast of experience since source could not know separateness without a physical reality or body. Apparently, this experiment ended in November 1989 when the last possible permutation and experience of separation took place, so then there was an energetic inquiry, the Harmonic Convergence, asking if our consciousness as a whole was ready for termination or graduation (sometimes referred to as ascension or enlightenment). To the surprise of all those who lovingly watch this planet of freewill express itself, as a whole, we were ready to graduate. Graduate status meant many changes, including diverting the asteroids coming our way, altering the magnetic grid, transferring the energies of sacred places back to humans, and since it was not necessary anymore, wrapping up karma (cause and effect), which appeared chaotic and sometimes violent. *The Indigo Children* information, the *Kryon* work, and Diana Cooper's books address much of this in detail. The bottom line is a big shift between the old energy consciousness and new energy consciousness as we rewrote our future in the shift of 2012. Guidance explained that before, those who chose not to awaken (muggles) were the majority, while the awakened (wizards) became the majority. Again, take it to your higher self and ask if you are interested. These changes were inspiring because they meant all problems have solutions, everyone can heal, all illness can be cured, and we can have it all: peace, love, joy, health, and prosperity. With all these changes that continue, it is necessary to have a conscious relationship with source because we would have experienced this level of transformation once we died, without a body and with the loving support of our soul families. There are infinite tools available to realize our partnership with pure consciousness, such as pendulums, qigong, meditation, and many more. Higher self consulting is a priceless direct tool due to its energetic and logical aspects.

Consider or remember the following information to expand your perception:

Your higher self does not judge. This source part of you is multi-dimensional and not subject to the limitations of the mind or polarity. Your choice of experience is honored —whether it is good or bad. Source energy communicates to everyone, from the Mother Teresas to Charles Mansons of the world, with the same unconditional love. We've all had hundreds of lifetimes —this means we have done it all. Everyone, at one point or another, murdered, raped, and pillaged. Your higher self will NEVER speak with judgment toward you. It may describe something someone is doing but will never judge you or judge anyone else. Once we die, our judgment, like our physical bodies, transform. I've spoken to many "dead" people while doing consultations, and it is always lovely and ego-free —as you will experience.

Events, challenges, and concepts are neutral; we assign them a positive or negative charge. Time challenges me sometimes. Even though time is neutral, our mind can use our perceived limitation of time to scare us into playing it safe and remaining habitual. Money is another popular trigger. Due to my extensive work here, lack of money challenged my faith. Since I'm aware of this past wound, I recognized it, felt the expansive feelings of my faith, and make conscious choices of abundance and prosperity.

Problems do not exist: they are all opportunities, and there is always a choice. Contrast is glorious. We all decide what we want to experience at the soul level, so we made some choices and continue to make new choices. We chose what we want to experience, a.k.a. major wounds, to deepen our experience throughout our lives. These wounds allow us to experience unconditional love, empowerment, wisdom, surrender, and so forth. We continue to choose how we experience our wounds in our playgrounds and theme parks of experience we call life. For example: if you chose forgiveness, you would require many people to forgive. We also chose our parents: usually to love us in a challenging way so we would take the individual's journey. Think about it; if we fit perfectly, we would have never left our nest and flown free. It is all a choice —all your choice. The good news is it continues to be your choice to do with it as you desire, and now you can work with it consciously and direct all your assistance to work with you.

You create your own reality. You **manifest** all the time, although you may not be aware of it. You are too powerful to entertain limiting thoughts. How we phrase all our thoughts and words is critical in our lives. Thoughts, feelings, and words manifest physically; tangible evidence is popping up all over the place. One of my favorites is Dr. Emoto's *The Hidden Messages in Water*, where he describes his work with water crystals. He exposes distilled water to words and then photographs the crystals, which form from exposure once the water is frozen. The images are startling. Sometimes they are beautiful, while at other times, crystals do not form. The images prove the power of thought and word with a visual representation of the word's intent or energy. Words we would not imagine as negative like the command "do it" are very different from their positive alternatives like "let's do it." The water crystals were featured in a very entertaining documentary called, *What the Bleep do We Know?* In which quantum physics is used to illustrate how we manifest. In *You Can Heal Your Life*, Louise L. Hay exposes the energetic cause of physical illness. Sometimes words are not enough; our greatest tool to manifesting consciously is our emotions. In *The Isaiah Effect*, Gregg Braden explores how feelings are the missing link and key to shifting our reality. When we're not aware of this, our underlying anxiety fortifies passing thoughts materializing our fear. To illustrate, a friend had the passing thought of what it would be like to side-swipe another car on the freeway; a week later, that is exactly what happened. It's okay to pontificate and consider all sorts of bizarre thoughts when you know that's all you're doing. The Universe wants to give you what you want, and it interprets what you want by your feel-

ings, which is why affirmations are not enough sometimes. The intent is everything. You can be saying: I am
grateful for perfect health while being afraid of getting
sick —that is what you can manifest when your fear is
stronger than your vision of health. This is why we must
focus on what we want. Another delicious resource for
manifesting is the Abraham-Hicks law of attraction material, called "deliberate creation."

Manifesting is different from control. The only thing
we control is our perception. We choose to interpret
everything as neutral, positive, or negative. It's up to us.
It's only a choice we make moment to moment. You are
real; everything else is an illusion. Essentially, we're all
delusional, so why not choose neutral or positive perceptions? Neutral means balance and allows us to experience the present time physically and unconditionally
in the emotional/spiritual sense. You will eventually be
disappointed with either positive or negative because in-
terpretations are not real and lead to suffering. Nevertheless, it is not productive to deny feelings, so it is best
to feel what is happening with full acceptance and then
choose how to use or change it to your ideal state.

We use many words and concepts habitually, and it's
valuable to break them down. Concepts like the difference between balance and harmony. What about the
word delusion? Love is neutral and the only non-delu-
sion. The delusion experience is relative or linear because to be delusional, we must be separate from reality.
Love is infinite and the only reality. So fear is actually

deluding our self from love. Deluding or moving away from love is the fear we experience. At the end of the day, everything is love and relative forms of love. Being uncomfortable, worried, and anxious is separation from love as well as the experience of disease. Love and its derivatives like joy and bliss are infinite. Our higher self's perception is infinite, while our human perception is limited because of the constraints of our limited physical body and perceived reality.

Source knows NO linear time; your higher self deals in and with the present time only. Keep your questions about the present and the very near future. I used to ask questions like, "At this time, how is my ego invested in me winning the bike race?" It's always "at this time." The **future** is always a probabilities game influenced by

Never assume. Never assume. Never assume. It is not our job to interpret; it is our job to ask. By taking communication at face value, we eliminate co-dependency. If we express ourselves and ask for clarification when we are confused, we alleviate passive-aggressiveness. At one point, although I do not remember my exact question, the guidance told me I was fearless. Fearless sounded great! I thought it meant I had no fear, which it did not. Now that I work on my awareness constantly, I realize I am afraid all the time. Nevertheless, I do it anyway: I act despite fear, nervousness, and anxiety. Had I asked more questions, I would have discovered that fear acts as a motivator in my playground. *The Four Agreements* by Don Miguel Ruiz is a lovely little book with a section about assumptions and explores how to transcend our matrix by changing the social and cultural agreements we were born into. He offers four new ones: be impeccable with your word, don't take anything personally, don't make assumptions, and always do your best. Though it sounds simple enough, the book is precious.

*Your higher self will **inform, not influence**.* Inform means to communicate knowledge, and influence means to affect, to alter, and to modify. The days of being separate from source are now over. The days of the superior and subordinate, master and pupil, or parent and child relationships are also over. All the divinity in the universe and all infinite power reside within each of your cells. You are infinite. There is no separation. You are an equal partner. Your higher self will NEVER tell you what to do. You make a choice, and only then —can it and will it— assist you in manifesting what you want. Initially, I wanted validation about whether or not I was on the right track. There is no right track; there is no wrong track— there is only your glorious track. Nothing you do or could do will set you off course. Like Abraham-Hicks says, "You never get it wrong, and you never get it done." No matter what challenges we face, we are NOT being punished. Nothing is happening to us; we are guiding it whether we realize it or not. This is so important to grasp. We have reached a time where awareness, feeling emotions, and self-expression are available and necessary for everyone who wants to continue with life experience. It's all a choice; there is no judgment. It's about taking responsibility and consciously participating in your life.

Shaun of the Dead is a funny zombie movie yet poignant because so many of us walk around on autopilot like the living dead. *Carpe Diem* —don't live like a zombie.

Joy is the marker. Joy is infinite. There is no such thing as a little joy; you either feel joy or you don't. Joy lets you know when you are in the flow, like surfing. Do you know the high surfers feel when they catch a wave? Think about all the moving elements when someone is surfing: the Earth, water, winds, themselves, and yet, they can balance with everything else and catch the flow —that's perfect mastery —in **real-time**.

Glossary

- Manifest: create, perceivable by the senses
- Future: probability, possible outcomes infinite possibilities. The guidance may tell you about an event but usually not the outcome. *The Present* by Spencer Johnson, M.D., is a charming short story about the present time.
- Inform: to communicate knowledge
- Influence: to affect or alter, to modify
- Carpe Diem: seize the day
- Real-time: present time, the moment

Chapter 8

Spiritual Laws

To live the metaphysical and wonder side of life, get very friendly with Universal Laws and use them consciously. Deepak Chopra and Diana Cooper have written books and articles about these Spiritual Laws in detail. The following are a taste of these laws and their relevance.

You are infinite—the real YOU, not your body. Your body is a finite expression of an infinite system; at the core, the body is made of energy, which cannot be created or destroyed. It's like the relative difference between three-dimensional thought and linear language. Thoughts, words, language, and fear are finite because they have a beginning and an end. Worry, fear, and doubt are finite; they are NOT infinite. Love is. Love is infinite. Joy is. Joy is infinite.

Please play by answering the following questions:

- Have you ever been in love? If not, felt love?

- What's the first love memory to pop up in your mind?

- How does it feel? Is it an expansive feeling? A feeling of freedom?

- Where in your body do you feel it? Is it localized?

- Where does that feeling come from?

That's right; it came from you: within you and available to you anytime, anywhere. That love you felt just now had nothing to do with the thing, person, or event you visualized. Whatever it was, it only triggered the love within you like a mirror allowing you to feel what was inside you all along. Do you have any idea of the energy it takes to shut it down? It's tremendous. You can create a trigger by touching your heart center, or wherever you feel love, to remind you of the TRUTH. You are love. You are infinite. This law is necessary to integrate and the missing piece for many people. Many have done all the work, read all the books, and yet they feel blah, disillusioned, and vulnerable. They don't understand why, so they judge themselves and beat themselves up internally for not being grateful or happy. Integrating this infinite idea forms a solid foundation in which to create.

When the self is taken care of, everything else is taken care of. Everything you do for yourself is an expression and measure of your love for yourself: how you eat, how you rest, how you exercise, your level of stress, and so forth. As a recovering workaholic, I know all about taking care of everything and everyone —except myself. I did not realize that everyone includes me. *The Mastery of Love* by Don Miguel Ruiz shines the light on unconditional love being an inside job —it starts within you, towards you, and afterward, we can share. One Minute for Yourself: A Simple Strategy for a Better Life by Spencer Johnson, M.D. is a tiny gem and grounded piece about taking care of ourselves. The Five Tibetans by Christopher S. Kilham is a little book about five rejuvenating and enriching yoga poses. These days I continuously ask myself what I am feeling instead of how I am feeling. When I rise in the morning, I also ask what my body requires as nourishment or exercise and what expression or play I require that moment or day. I then ask my higher self other questions or to help me prioritize my day.

As within, so without: people mirror what's happening to us and reveal parts of ourselves. We are one. We are connected by source, the Akashic Records, our archetypes, and much more. Alone, we can fool ourselves and dwell in denial since we are our own blind spot. Living with a partner allows us to see what we're denying. Love and Awakening: Discovering the Sacred Path of Intimate

Relationship by John Welwood illuminates the mirror principle in detail.

The Law of Projection states that everything is a reflection: things and events mirror our inner world. Unity means there is no separation. How we do one thing is how we do everything. When we look in the mirror, we don't change the reflection; we change ourselves. With martial arts, you can experience many of these ideas, which we can't usually see. A dear friend, Sifu Marcus, taught Jeet Kune Do (JKD) and Qigong, and other disciplines. Bruce Lee developed JKD because he wanted an art, which mimics life instead of a non-organic system; his motto was, "Use no way as way and having no limitation as your only limitation." Eventually, my sister and I took his class. By observing how we hit a pad, he broke down our defense mechanisms and how they were affecting the rest of our lives. I saw how I habitually over-controlled and hyperextended, which hurt me because I was not relating to the person or situation in front of me. Funny enough, I tried to overpower them – I'm only 5'3", so everyone who trained with me was bigger and stronger. My sister tended to withdraw; fortunately, nothing brings you into the moment like getting hit in the face. I trained for about a year, which was challenging because I was not fit or coordinated, and then stopped. About a year later, I returned and hit a pad to see if I could remember how to do it. To my surprise, I hit harder and much more dynamically because I spent that year doing internal work. When your martial arts get better, your life gets better; your martial arts get better when your life gets better. This applies to everything we do. There is no separation.

The Law of Attraction: like attracts like. If you want more love, be more loving. Getting the Love You Want by Harville Hendrix, Ph.D. explores why we attract the people in our lives and how to create harmony with them.

The Law of Abundance: it is your birthright to be healthy and prosperous. Secrets of the Millionaire Mind: Mastering the Inner Game of Wealth by Harv T. Eker exposes how our limiting beliefs affect our capacity to create wealth and maintain it.

We are not alone: everyone has a team of unseen assistance on many levels. Source, your higher self, and the Akashic Records are a part of this group and give us access to anyone who ever lived or is alive now. When I directed my first film, I called upon two directors (one who did not have a physical body and another who still did) to energetically be with me while we shot. I might have asked only one question, yet the support was priceless. It was easy and fun to direct though I had never done it before and was under immense constraints. Did their assistance make the difference between success or failure? I never asked. They gave me courage like a lifeline you can reach for if you wish.

"Ask, and you shall receive" is how we enact our freewill. Nothing can happen without our permission, and our direction, which is why asking questions is so important.

Be, Do, Have is the order of things. Most people wait to have before doing anything. Instead, we must be it, do it, to have it. The Harv T. Eker book discusses this law, and in Leslie Fieger's Delfin Knowledge System, also known as the *Master Key System*, he describes this and the other Universal Laws in detail while connecting spiritual and scientific facts.

Everything is moving and, consequently, fluid. Our inability to flow and be fluid determines the resistance we experience and how often we bump into things. *Who Moved my Cheese?* by Spencer Johnson, M.D. is another gem about change. Though it applies to everything, Leslie Fieger gives an analogy about money in the Delfin work. He describes money as a flowing stream from which we can get a cup full, a bucket full, swim in, and even build a water wheel for power —as long as we do not stop the flow. Martial arts are also an excellent way to experience the importance of being in the flow physically.

Keep in mind inclusivity, a.k.a. the both-concept or the all-concept. This is related to the truth within a paradox. A paradox takes us off balance so we can find balance. There are infinite possibilities in our lives, yet we continuously try and compartmentalize to an either-or scenario. It is not necessary to only feel one emotion. It's not about one or the other; it's both because everything can exist simultaneously in this infinite universe. We can be angry and compassionate, serious and funny, spiritual and rich, or friends and work together professionally. We get in trouble when we pretend we can only experience one thing at a time. Have you ever read a great novel and wanted to know what happens in the end, yet you did not want the book to end so you could savor every word? This is the both-concept, which is actually the all-concept because the polarity of both is too limiting. Accepting our physical and metaphysical nature is a necessary part of awareness and self-knowledge. It is a paradox of being a part of the source and the whole universe while also being an individual.

Glossary

- Fluid: subject to change or movement, characterized by a smooth easy style
- Flow: to easily move in continual change
- Paradox: seemingly contradictory ideas

Chapter 9

Common Themes

After so many professional consultations and so much personal work, some common themes have come to light. These topics are useful to explore once you start working directly with your higher self. Including:

Glorious living: Your birthright. There is nothing wrong with you. You are too glorious for limitations and suffering.

Wonder: Spirit expressed and the link to love and metaphysics.

Wellness: The ideal expression of the body and its ability to heal.

Wisdom: The ultimate expression of the mind and ability to discern qualities and relationships synergistically and in the moment – not about accumulating facts.

Acceptance: Honoring yourself and letting go of judgment about you and everyone else.

Awareness: Increasing your perception and knowledge. Experiencing and expressing yourself in real-time.

Empowerment: Increasing your self-actualization and influence – not as in control, which is limited. Empowerment is expansive.

Unconditional Love: Neutrality, the ability to feel your truth and express it. *Universal Compassion: Transforming Your Life through Love and Compassion* by Geshe Kelsang Gyatso discusses how to tap into infinite love.

Peace: Your inner state of tranquility and security, freedom from disquieting or oppressive thoughts or emotions, and harmony in personal relationships.

Detachment: Freedom from bias or prejudice, which does not mean indifference. Attachment causes our suffering, which is the difference between our expectations and reality. The problem is the expectation and our attachment to it. Like Buddha said, "Pain is inevitable, suffering is optional."

Surrender: The acceptance of your infinite nature. Surrender is not a weakness or giving up as it is assumed physically. In metaphysical terms, surrendering does not mean giving in to an external force or object. It means letting go of the resistance to your higher self. Surrender is always empowering; it never makes you less than whole, weak, or disempowered. As the saying goes, "you must empty your cup before you can fill it" or "the closed hand does not receive." Lack of perception of the true self is what slows you down or gets in your way. By accepting and surrendering to who you truly are, you expand. The race to have more power is, by definition, finite because it has a beginning and end. On the other hand, surrender is infinite, as we can always surrender more. In Qigong, the concept of surrender is defined by the principle that we can always relax more. Any power you can conceive of is always less than the power you truly are and the power you possess. To realize and cultivate it, we must surrender to it.

New Paradigm: The new consciousness, which is evolving and we are collectively designing.

Other Lifetimes (also referred to as past lives): *Archetypes* or actual experiences from other times. Other lives only come up when something about it is holding you back. The key to harmonizing these memories is forgiveness. Usually, we were very upset about the circumstance, the situation, or the people we left behind at the time of our death, so the guidance allows us to see what happened from an expansive perspective. With this new point of view, we can accept the sequence of events and forgive ourselves. It's always very healing to cry in the loving energy of your higher self if you feel compelled; there are healing and information stored in our bodies, which can only be released through our tears.

Our Gift to the World (sometimes referred to as our purpose, mission, dharma, or primary archetype): We are all here to be human, divine expressions of source, and contribute. Most possess one predominantly gift, which gets expressed in many ways and on many levels. When I first asked about my mission, I assumed it meant career, but the Records said it had to do with unconditional love and creativity. This wasn't very clear because I also assumed anything to do with love was about romantic love. It took about four years to get clear on all this because I had much to discover about myself, what these concepts actually meant, and how to phrase and ask more specific questions.

Caroline Myss' *Sacred Contracts* allowed me to narrow down my primary archetypes since I oscillated between storyteller and teacher. Through a workshop I developed to identify one's life's purpose, I figured out: I was an awakener/teacher, and storyteller was one way my teacher expressed. On reviewing my entire life, I understood I was always teaching though it was mostly unconscious and took many forms and shapes. As a kid, I would learn something and regurgitate it to anyone who would listen. As an adolescent, I expressed myself through writing; as a teenager, I counseled all my friends. My love of learning got me three bachelor, two Masters, and a Doctorate. As a filmmaker, I focused on educating everyone I worked with; I explained every detail while only working on entertaining and empowering material. I did not realize that my need to help others recognize their empowerment meant teaching. Because I did not perfectly fit the ideas I had about teachers, and since I was not the one-on-one type, I assumed the teacher could not be it and rejected it. I had to accept I was unconventional and a teacher nonetheless. Eventually, I embraced it and taught through counseling, writing, food, and business with the subjects of empowerment, self-expression, vibrant health, spiritual partnership, and more. Now that I am teaching consciously, I am expressing my gift fully.

Once I accepted that I am a teacher and surrendered to it, my life changed. I wasn't going against the current anymore; it got me in the flow. It gave me clarity and the ability to apologize to my family because I finally understood why they felt I was controlling – I was teaching people who were NOT my students and did not ask! It gave me the freedom to stop judging my process and myself. I realized why I was so different from most of my friends. I recognized that as artists, facilitators, and nurturers, it was not necessary for them to keenly observe everything and translate it to others as I do. For instance, while speaking to my late mother one day, she asked me about my sister. So, I answered and shared my thoughts, which tend to be detailed and deep. Then, sarcastically with the usual ", you think you know everything" tone, she said something about me always playing the analytical psychologist. For the first time, I was not offended. I calmly replied, "Exactly, that is what I do. As a teacher, I cannot help noticing behavior and patterns. It is my job to name these things and interpret them." She replied, "Oh, okay," and the conversation moved on in a light and surprising way. I was thrilled because accepting my inner teacher also allowed me to communicate compassionately with the most challenging people in my life.

Embracing myself as an awakener has opened up so many opportunities and abundance. I used to think I was so spread out with spirituality, movies, business, learning, and everything else when my life was simply about awakening. Even resting and proper nourishment is essential to my teaching. Recognizing it is ALL the same, has relieved so much of my anxiety, allowing me to feel peace and truly express myself. Awakening/teaching is my gift to the world and my playground for growth. The first time I asked, "What is blocking me from my mission?" My guidance let me know the only thing in my way was myself because I felt I had to do everything first before expressing it to others —they told me not to wait; I had no idea what they were actually talking about at the time. My ability to awaken/teach, like your gift, is innate; therefore, you know you're experiencing it when life is easy, has no resistance, and is harmonious. I still get nervous, but the opportunities to express my gifts constantly appear.

Healing: This is an inside job – it manifests from within you. It cannot happen unless you want it to. There are benefits we get from illness, and it helps us to be aware of what they are to increase our healing options. For example, I knew a woman who was diagnosed with Multiple Sclerosis. She was able to rehabilitate her paralysis and able to walk. People noticed her slight limp, opened doors for her, and gave her positive attention, more attention than when she was not ill. She had managed her disease to a point where the attention pays off was better than complete healing.

Tune in to quantum healing. Healing can take a second, two minutes, two years, or a lifetime; it is up to you. Keep in mind: Everything happens for your benefit based on your design. Actually, things happen for a good reason, and it's more like MANY reasons. The Universe is very efficient; each event fulfills many purposes.

A dear friend was so stubborn that it took kidney failure to get him to wakeup. He was already meditating, exercising, and eating well —he was the healthiest person I knew. He went from being an athlete to not being able to move and in torturous pain. One day, he thought he had stomach flu because he could not eat or drink anything and was throwing up none stop. Once the doctors saw his blood results, they panicked and asked him how he was still conscious because he had the chemistry of a person who had battery acid for blood. They then discovered that his kidneys did not work and probably had not worked for a long time though he had no obvious symptoms until three days earlier. He was told he would have to give up martial arts, his number one passion, and what he thought was his purpose in life. He would have to have his blood filtered for three hours, three times per week forever. He had to restrict his water intake to three glasses a day, could not eat fruit, vegetables, or whole grain. He would lose his memory, some sight, and hearing. His bones would become brittle, and he would lose some of his teeth. He'd be anemic and weak for the rest of his life, dependent on medication forever, and much more. The doctors told him all this was painful but manageable and gave him seven to twelve years to live. He'd arrived at the hospital four days after his twenty-sixth birthday. After hearing his death sentence, he eventually broke down and cried for about a week. He was in excruciating pain and eventually noticed that it got worse when he focused on his pain. So there he was at the lowest of lows in a cycle of depression staring out a window into a courtyard with one pitiful tree. The tree reminded him of nature, and he felt slightly better for the first time since he got ill. Consequently, he decided to gaze outside again and then noticed the sunshine, realizing that what he focused on expanding. Eventually, with this process, he took full responsibility for his power, which led him to understand his role in his own suffering. He decided to never participate in his or anyone else's suffering ever again and never let anyone else participate with him or for him, which led him to have the strength to disagree with all his doctors, find another way, and choose life. He had no idea there was another way and took the ride anyway because he knew any alternative was better than suffering. He had more than twenty near-death experiences and surrendered through each one. Each time deepening his awareness, expanding his compassion and joy for life. For twenty years, he was on peritoneal dialyzes and in pain but did not suffer. In fact, he thrived, enjoyed every day, and did not empower his challenge. He vigorously practiced martial arts and ate whatever he wanted and understood was best for him. If you looked at him, you would have never known he had kidney problems because he was healthy and energetic. He was also a teacher, personal trainer, and health and nutrition consultant. I illustrate part of his journey because he credited his kidney limitations with inspiring his awakening. If he had not experienced this, he would not have consciously and purposefully helped as many people as he did.

Chapter 10

Available Answers

"Successful people ask better questions, and as a result, they get better answers." ~ *Tony Robbins*

The answers to our questions and request for guidance are always there and available. Our receptivity can get cloudy, and our questions require empowerment and specificity. It is always possible to deepen the conversation when coming from an empowered co-creative partnership and clear questions.

Everyone feels the energy of their higher self once they recite the Key. The ability to discern between your thoughts and information from pure consciousness may take practice —mostly the practice of asking questions. Let's walk through a consultant-client session as practice because you will act as your own consultant.

Though ninety-nine percent of the harmonizing and healing is energetic and one percent verbal, higher self consultations begin with the consultant and client sitting face-to-face, unless it's over the phone or video chat. They sit across from each other because the information comes in through the crown **chakra** (top of head) and is delivered through the heart chakra (center). They have both feet flat on the ground with their arms uncrossed, not interrupting the energy flow. The consultant may look up at a blank wall or the open sky now and again until the information becomes seamless in real-time. All along, it appears as if the consultant is speaking.

Initially, a consultation starts with the client discussing their situation, like stating their case in court, so source energy can comment on the information to shed any misperceptions before addressing the questions. Often, the concern or issue gets resolved before getting to the questions.

Internally, the consultant is having a parallel conversation with the higher self of the client in silence, asking other questions to **calibrate** and verify the information such as:

- What do you have to say about what they are saying?

- Is this (their perception) accurate?

- Are you sure?

- Is this (coming from) you or me? Most of the time they answer "us" or "We're in agreement. Keep going."

When I feel I'm off on a tangent, I ask to calibrate:

- Is this appropriate (to share with this person)?

The answer is usually "yes" because they use all our experience to help others, but I keep asking just in case. I've included these questions to use for yourself as your own consultant and to calibrate throughout your practice.

- Chakras: centers of spiritual power in the human body
- Calibrate: to test and adjust the accuracy of a process

When I've asked, "Why me? Why am I a valuable facilitator for this work?" They've said that on one level, I agreed to. More specifically, due to my capacity to awaken, teach, and because of my personal desire to be of service, I have the ability to get out of the way. My commitment and intention are for the greatest benefit of the client. I always state, "If I say anything inappropriate, please stop me." I'm not there for my benefit. It is all about the individual in front of me; I'm here to serve. A lot of stuff comes through me, which I don't understand, so I ask the person:

- Does this make sense? Do you get it?

- If anything is not clear, we can ask for clarification or ask them to explain it in another way.

Somehow, the person understands, so I keep going even if I don't. I also do not remember the details of the consultations; usually, I remember the overall feeling of it, which is always a beautiful experience. As your own consultant, it is helpful to journal your consultations to refer to your notes. I also suggest you pretend to be someone else taking the stance of an objective reporter doing an interview.

Regarding answers, keep in mind:
Ninety-nine percent of the harmonizing or healing is energetic, and one percent is verbal. Your words direct; source's words make us feel nice and help our brains catch up.

Your higher self provides direction, no judgment like right or wrong. Because there are infinite possibilities, there is never just one reason for anything and never just one answer. It's about the answers, which lead us to realization and self-actualization. The film The Matrix illustrates this beautifully with the Oracle character. Because there is no right or wrong, the information is simply direction leading us on a pathway to express ourselves and create. Freewill is the law and extremely important because nothing can happen without our permission. In the movie, Neo, Keanu Reeve's character, went to ask the Oracle if he was the One. She asked him what he thought and told him, "Know Thyself." At that point, he was not the one because he did not believe he was. The Oracle told him what he needed to hear; therefore, releasing the pressure and allowing him to become the One. This higher self consulting and Akashic Records metaphor also extended to the second film, The Matrix Reloaded, when the Oracle tells Neo that he's already made his choice; he's there to find out why he made it. This is how it works.

I have a personal and expensive example of how this can play out. Remember when I was told a better job opportunity would come along and take it? It did, and I took it because it felt right. I was not afraid because I remembered what they said. So, I left a chaotic but well-paying job to create a new production company and make a few low budget independent movies with ten million dollars. I was ecstatic about my new opportunity and felt grateful someone was finally giving me a real chance. Translation: low self-esteem, low self-worth, and no awareness of my true value —all of which create disharmony. Unfortunately, the investor misled me to believe the deal was solid. Eager to start, I floated

the company's expenses, hired a writer, and began lo-
cation scouting in Ireland, all with the understanding I
would be reimbursed. I was busy producing while we experienced delays with the funding. Six months later, it
became clear the deal was not happening. Even though
I was a hundred thousand dollars in debt due to this
ordeal, I was never reimbursed and eventually had to
sell my condo and file for bankruptcy. On paper, my
life looked suicidal. This period was very challenging,
physically, professionally, emotionally, and spiritually.
Through this experience, I learned many priceless
lessons and started getting my power back. You may
be wondering why they led me down this path? Yes, it
sucked, but I eventually understood. At the soul level,
I had set up money obstacles to get my attention and
wake me up from my denial of self. I used to be very re-
actionary, letting the victim archetype run my life, wondering why things happened to me. I also realized intent
and truth were singular, so my intention to create my
reality and be a victim could not coexist. Had the deal
gone through, it would have taken me a very long time to
wake up spiritually and move towards my true self. Even
though I thought the guidance got me in that mess, I was
grateful to be able to feel their love and speak with them
about what was happening. I cannot say it was easy, but
it was worth it.

*Your higher self will not give you information or lead
you in a direction you cannot handle.* We've agreed to

let them assist us once we're ready. Everyone is infinite. You are infinite and with your full awareness; that means you are infinite plus one, while most people run around unaware of themselves with their infinite glory like a hidden treasure. With this tool, you become infinite, plus one (your higher self), including infinite knowledge —there is nothing you cannot handle. Just ask for assistance and guidance.

When consulting your higher self, you may journal, speak, scream, or debate with them like one of my friend's grandmother used to. Be careful with screaming out loud because some people may not understand; however, your higher self does not mind.

Everyone receives guidance differently: some hear it, see it, feel it, or know it. Initially, some hear pure consciousness in their own voice, though it may eventually change to a different tone. I get a combination. When I see, the images are like an invisible hologram or memory. When I hear them, it has always been in my voice. Even when talking to "dead" people, they sound like me; however, they have a distinctive speaking style or use words I would not normally use. While working on my friend Asya's biography, I suggested we speak to her grandmother Hana directly to hear what she had to say since we were writing about her life. Hana is the grandmother who used to yell at source. So, I accessed Asya's higher self and asked if Hana was available. To my surprise, my friend was able to speak directly with Hana in Arabic. It was fascinating. When you speak to Masters like Buddha or famous people like Frank Sinatra or Oprah Winfrey, you'll probably hear them in their voice.

When I speak to source, I do not ask them to identify themselves or call in a specific Master unless I do research. Since I did not have a religious or spiritual upbringing, I did not form relationships with any Masters before working with the Akashic Records. Now, however, I know they are all there. If you grew up praying to Mother Mary, talk to her and explore the other entities. Stay open, and let it flow.

Source communicates your way. I have a brilliant friend, David, who has a very complex mind; when source speaks through him, he is the only one who understands. I have several friends who do not require a Key to access their higher selves because they consciously communicate all the time. Though one of them is a very peaceful man, they speak to him straightforwardly, like his inner monologue.

Source is literal. Do not take language for granted —ask. I had a consultation where they told my client a particular doctor would be available. What does available actually mean? Energetically and/or physically? I have no idea what they meant; we could have asked.

Another example is when I moved from Miami to Los Angeles, and I wasn't sure whether to fly or drive. I had the opportunity to buy a new Ford Explorer without any money down. My friend, Andrea, who I was going with, was concerned about the car's safety while I felt safe. I asked and got, "It does not matter which you choose; you will not be hurt." Afterward, while driving to LA two hours north of Miami, we stopped for gas and switched drivers. Andrea drove out of the rest stop during morning rush hour traffic, lost control of the car, and we did cartwheels on the highway as we rolled over quite dramatically. The car was totaled, and we were not hurt. The guidance did not say I would not get in an accident, though I assumed hurt and accidents went together. Later, they clarified the experience was so Andrea could recognize her power to manifest and be aware of the thoughts she empowers. The accident allowed me to release my delusions concerning my father —emotionally painful yet necessary for me to leave with a clean slate, see my father as a human being, and be free.

Whether visual, written, or auditory, answers may be one word or a huge sermon. I usually ask, "What would you have me know today?" These tend to be simple answers or no answers because the question may be too general, while others get book-length material. If we ask vague questions, we get vague answers. If you begin with a "yes" or "no" question, don't stop there. Keep going with more questions to create a conversation.

Always acknowledge: write down or say the first thing you hear/see/realize to get the momentum flowing. Start with whatever comes up first because it usually leads to much more.

Follow the flow. The first answer is like turning on the computer, the second is like opening the web browser, the third is like going to google, the fourth is reading the search results, and the rest of the answers are what you learn about the topic.

Answers may be subtle. I've noticed in consultations when the person asking is triggered, their perception is just one notch off on the harmony dial. Even though it may be tiny, the disparity has a great consequence. Fortunately, it does not take much to correct the disharmony. Usually, an open heart with healing intent harmonizes quickly.

Answers are for the present time only. Asking the same question usually yields a different answer because everything, including our perception, is fluid and constantly changing.

Sometimes source does not answer and always with good reason. The question may be vague, or they may want you to rephrase it due to limiting language. There may be no energy for that subject, or it may be irrelevant. That is, if I ask, "Was I, Cleopatra?" It may not matter and is of no consequence even if I was Cleopatra unless that lifetime held me back right now. At other times, we're in the middle of an epiphany or lesson. Note that epiphanies may take a long time to materialize completely, and a lesson implies experience —not punishment. Our higher self cannot do the work for us; nevertheless, we can always ask:

- Why can't I hear you?

- Is it best to rephrase the question?

- Is _____ relevant?

- Am I in it (in the midst of an epiphany)?

- What can you tell me about it?

- What is most important about this dynamic for me to know?

- How will I feel once I've cleared this?

With practice, you will be able to differentiate between your opinion and source guidance. I have a friend who has had a very long and challenging relationship, which has been an incredible source of love and growth. As her friend, I had consulted on her behalf on many occasions. Eventually, my opinion became crystal clear:

she should drop him and move on! Regardless, we'd take it to source to find out what was really going on. In the energy, I could feel their connection, and their potential was glorious. We'd usually ask, "Has the relationship run its course?" and the answer was usually no; even though, both had to choose a sacred partnership for their liaison to move to another level. Be clear when you ask such a question and all questions. This question leaves a lot of room for interpretation: Which course were they still on since we know love is infinite and on which level or realm? My friend did so much work with her guidance about this relationship; she would discuss it with many consultants. One day she worked with a new one who was not experienced. She called me up to go in to find out what went wrong because they both left the session bewildered. Every time we asked, "Has it run its course?" we heard a "no." The new consultant heard, "yes," which sent my friend into shock, made the consultant nervous, and the whole thing fell apart. So we went in to find out what happened or what changed. Their relationship was in a very negative place, and this phase had run its course. In fact, things had to change to keep going, which my friend was well aware of. The lesson is not to let the first answer derail you from going deeper and getting clarity. Never end a session if you feel any disharmony or any confusion. They may not tell you exactly what you want to hear, but they will support you if and when you ask.

The answers will one day be an integrated part of your being and your expression as they are for me today.

Chapter 11

Every Consult

The Protocol

The following steps will be part of the process every time you consult for yourself.

How to prepare for your higher self consultation:

1. Set your overall intention for the session. ***
2. Write down your questions and intention for each one, if applicable. ?/*
3. Use the Key to access your higher self. #
4. State your case to shine divine light on it so that your guides can comment and correct any mis-perceptions. !
5. Ask your questions and explore them. ?

6. Exit when done. |

7. Ground yourself. _

Symbols can act as abbreviations when you journal. You can use these or choose your own.

*** Overall intention

* Intention

The Key

! State your case

? Questions

| Exit

_ Ground

Chapter 12

Word Choice

To recap: everyone is divine, you are divine, and all is within you. Source will not interfere with free will; therefore, we have to direct the assistance your energetic team provides. The healing/shift begins with you creating your questions.

Words are like spells loaded with assumptions and limitations, so be aware of which words you use and how you use them. There are distinctions between: need, require, and next steps towards. Keep in mind the difference between asking "How can I...." and "How do I...".

I spoke about the gratitude I felt for a past relationship, and I said the relationship was extraordinary. They corrected me and let me know not to empower that it was extra-ordinary. They let me know glorious was a more accurate description because it allowed my relationship to be ordinary and honored at the same time (the both/all concept). The same care must be taken with all our language and thoughts. Monitoring our thoughts can be an interesting experiment. One day, I decided to monitor myself and release every non-supportive thought over to the light. It was an avalanche of negativity the entire day; I walked around saying to myself, "I turn it over to the light, I turn it over to the light." Fortunately, I did not judge it, and it passed after emptying my mind of all the limiting thoughts I had not expressed. It was like fasting for the mind where I could detox my repressed negativity because my intent was release. Many times we have to remove the garbage so the beauty can be expressed.

Chapter 13

Intent

Your intent is everything. The intention is the difference between an enlightening charm and a wicked curse. Stating your desires and goals before making your inquiry is a powerful way to direct reality and your higher self. Intentions may shift as you ask different questions. You may have an overall intention such as *** Glorious Living and have specific intentions for each question like * Wellbeing when asking, "What's most important about a morning ritual?" Then * Wonder, while asking, "What your priority for play is?" Possible intentions will be listed in the Practice Exercises.

Here are some suggestions:

* To express all the glory that I am

* To live the most glorious life possible

* Because I'm to glorious to suffer/to deal with drama

* To express and experience unconditional love

*To live the truth of my glorious being

* To express and experience compassion

* Free of fear / Celebrate fear

* Dissolve my limitations / Expand awareness

* Glorious Living / Experience harmony

* Experience intimacy / Honor intimacy

* Expand awareness / Celebrate awareness

* Clarity / Understanding

* Wonder / Express joy

* Assist without taking responsibility

* Assist for everyone's highest good

* Assist without getting involved in other people's karma

* Wellness / Healing

* Confirmation

* Settle negative feelings

* Use my archetypes in positive ways

* Harmony / Integration

* Wisdom / Truth

* Connection

* Get out of my own way / Surrender

* Allowing / Greater ability to receive

Chapter 14

State Your Case

We show up full and loaded. We are filled with ideas and perceptions about everything. Since everyone has center of the universe disease, let's acknowledge and view our points of view, so they do not hold us back.

When consulting for yourself, you want to start by setting an intention so your guidance can help you manifest what you want. Then you state your case to describe your perspective to get clarification and expand your perception before asking your questions.

Think about declaring what you think, believe, and where you stand at the moment, like stating your case as you would in a court of law so that your understanding is clear and your higher self can set you straight, per se. Stating your perception/opinion about a relationship or situation before getting to your questions will ensure your accuracy. With greater objectivity, we can adjust our questions accordingly.

These are some examples of how to phrase your case:

! I believe _____. Please comment on my perception?

! My understanding is _____. How are my personal filters affecting this?

! Is _____ accurate?

! Is _____ appropriate and in alignment with _____ desire/intention?

! What false beliefs am I operating from if any?

! How am I motivated by my personality/ego?

! What else about this story do I need to know/understand/let go of?

Come back to this once your Wizard awakens.

Chapter 15

Wizarding Guidelines

Ready, Set, Magic!

The Key is sacred and a blessing to you. Protect it and carry a copy with you at all times; it is your Key. Never copy the directions on the same page as the Key. I do not believe anyone could actually cause harm with this tool; however, I do know it won't be very clear if one has not read all of this or taken a class because source communicates through light and sound. This training calibrates you and gives you the necessary integrated translation system to interpret their data. I've met so many ready people; unfortunately, it would have been irresponsible to hand over the Key without giving them proper instruction.

NO recreational drugs or alcohol 24 hours before accessing your higher self directly. Prescription medications are acceptable. Use your discretion with heavy pain medications; you can always ask once you're in. This is not about morality or ethics; it is because these substances interfere with our energy field. We want our fields to be pristine and intact because when it's compromised, it feels confusing and may lead to misinterpretation.

Preparation: You will require a journal, notebook, or tablet to write longhand with. Prepare for your session by writing out your questions on a separate piece of paper so you can refer to it without flipping pages. Plus, once you're in, it feels good, so it's easy to get distracted and forget what you wanted to ask. Get ready in whatever way you like as long as it clears the mind. Quiet your mind, take a few deep breaths, do a tuning exercise, meditate, light a candle, call in the light, or whatever you like. Finally, sit in a comfortable position and don't cross your legs or arms since this tends to interrupt the energy flow; though, some yogis can sit in lotus without interrupting the flow.

Always read the Key; it is not to be changed. If opened from memory, it is possible to miss or change a word. Eventually, you may not need to say the Key to communicate with your higher guidance. Though I do not require it anymore, I say it anyway because it is sacred, the ritual strengthens intent, and the words are a beautiful reminder of what's really real. When doing a consultation, I use another Key to do higher self consultations for others, which is not listed here, as it is advanced wizardry.

Eyes open, looking up. It helps to look at a blank wall or open sky. Keep eye closing to a minimum to avoid trance channeling. Some people feel they will hear better or see clearer with their eyes closed; this is a habitual response and not necessary. We are operating with a fully conscious mind.

DO NOT drive a car or use heavy machinery while the key has been activated and the field is open.

Use good judgment when deciding how long to stay in direct source energy. One must build a tolerance to the energy. You can go in anytime and anywhere. Use good judgment when deciding how long to stay in. You can do anything like go to the bathroom, eat, and even use inappropriate language; they do not judge and have a sense of humor. Once you get comfortable, explore, and experiment with such activities as having sex or taking a nap while in activated source energy. I do not recommend sleeping with your source guidance activated as it can be too distracting.

The Key does the work; the words, said in the right order, work on everyone – whether they believe or not. It is necessary to practice asking questions and hearing/seeing/realizing answers to get used to it and develop the sensitivity to understand when it's source, you, your *inner child*, or your mind/ego communicating. Trust you are in and do not edit. When journaling, write everything down to review later. Respond to all information given or all experiences while you are in.

Get your hand moving by rewriting the question. This will kick start the process. Most of the time, you'll hear, feel, or know your answers before you're finished writing out the question. If you do not, be patient and continue working with it. It can help to get your pen moving with squiggly lines to allow the words to come through.

Be curious, open, and kind. Socrates said, *"All I know is I know nothing."* Having an objective, clear, and open approach will allow you to access greater depth and information. Approach it objectively like a professional investigative reporter with some unconditional love. I like to think of the Dalai Lama conducting an interview. Remember they are here to inform, not influence. Do NOT assume and do NOT interpret; you are to ASK and ASK, and then ASK again for clarification.

Ground yourself after each time you have been in. Go outside, walk barefoot, exercise, eat root vegetables, eat chocolate, have sex, wear black socks, visualize yourself like a tree growing roots in the ground, declare, "I am grounded," and so on.

Only consult for others when asked and with clear consent. There is a different Key; however, you can access infinite knowledge through your higher self. For instance, you may get painting lessons from Salvador Dalí or speak to Merlin about new charms. You can also help assist your friends. Let's say someone you know has a problem; once you let him or her know that you have a magical oracle-like ability, and they say they would like to ask a question. They have permitted you to ask, so you can go into yours and speak to your higher self on their behalf, ask the question, and hear/see what guidance is provided.

Though Yoli insisted I get a consultation, I do not recommend this approach. It is appropriate to invite and give your friends the room to accept, which will not create co-dependency. When appropriate, let people know you're working with some great stuff and that you are available to explore their situation, allowing them to step up if and when they are ready. If they request that you ask something on their behalf, you will say everything you see and everything you hear. Remember, this work is about empowerment, not confusion. If they look confused, ask for help and clarity. Problems can arise when the initial communication is not what the friend was expecting and tenses up, making a novice consultant nervous and more susceptible to interpretation or shut down. I find it is best to practice with fun questions of no consequence initially.

Consulting for others takes practice. Many times, beginners cannot consult for other people because if they did, they would skip over themselves and start spreading the love; consequently, they avoid their personal work. It may take time before you can assist your friends directly. Once you complete all the exercises in this training and you feel comfortable working, I suggest you introduce this work to a close friend so they can take the class and you can become Consulting Partners after they have taken Level 1. At the end of this course, you'll find an agreement to facilitate this partnership process.

Do not give or teach the Key to anyone without proper training. People come to this work when they are ready, which is why you took this class and signed your Wizarding Registration Agreement. This multilevel ritual ensures you want this, are ready for it, and value it. Sharing this text is not appropriate, either. It is important to give your friends the space to step forward and take a class to express their intent and start the magical process physically. Feel free to share the other Charms or tools within the material.

Age and maturity levels are important. How young can someone be to consult their own higher self directly? Sixteen is the recommendation. Parents are connected to their children and can consult through their own source on their behalf. When in doubt: just ask your guidance.

Chapter 16

The Magic Key

"Give a man a fish and you feed him for a day; teach a man how to fish and you feed him for a lifetime." ~ *Anonymous*

The Key for Higher Self Consulting

The Magic Key is:

> "Higher self of MY soul,
> I access thee for MY growth."

~~~~~~

Glossary

Higher self: Your true metaphysical nature, source energy, God, Akashic Records, Ascended masters, teachers and loved ones, zero-point energy

Soul: individual; your independent part of source expressing itself through this life and others; the complex of human attributes that manifest as consciousness, thought, feeling, and will, regarded as distinct from the physical body

Access: the opportunity to experience or make use of

MY: belonging to the whole, which includes you, everyone else, the planet, and Source

Growth: the processes of developing and expanding expression

.

The Incantation

To access your higher self and the Akashic Records, you will read the Key twice: first, out loud, exactly as it is written, and the second, to yourself without speaking, in silence, while replacing the word "my" with your legal first and last name in the possessive tense. Your legal name is written on your driver's license or passport today; it is unnecessary to use your middle name. Fill in your legal first and last name on the blank lines below.

In its entirety, the Key reads as follows:

Out loud:

"Higher self of MY soul,
I access thee for MY growth."

In silence:

"Higher self of _____'s soul,
I access thee for _____'s growth."

Take a moment to feel the shift.

How do you feel? What difference did you experience?

After taking sensory inventory of the shift, ask out loud: "Am I in?"

Did something happen? What did you hear, see, feel, or know?

Once you have felt the shift, you can exit.

To exit, deactivate, or close out, say out loud: "Thank you. Thank you. Thank you."

Once you close, check if you are in by asking, "Am I in?"

You are now an *Awakened Wizard!* You can now use this tool as needed. You get to choose when you are in and out.

If you are not clear, try it again. If having trouble, see the Troubleshooting section. Every single student I have ever had has been able to experience it. It may take going in and out a few times to get used to the experience. Be patient and gentle with yourself.

Printed Magic Key cards are available at macare-naluzb.com with the password: Wombat.

Practice Exercises

"Knowledge is of no value unless you put it into practice." ~ Anton Chekhov

The following exercises are designed to get you to feel and experience the difference between your opinions and your higher self consulting. Keep it light so you can practice. You can always do these with more important topics at a later time.

Take your time exploring them, and have patience with yourself as you practice.

Have something to write on. You want to write in cursive unless you can type faster.

Chapter 17

Nothing is Random

Exercise 1

Nothing is random. *Everything happens for your benefit,* so most things have several good reasons for participating with you.

1. Get a deck of cards – any deck. It does not matter whether it is a poker or tarot deck.

2. Shuffle the cards and lay them out face down.

3. Pick one, turn it over, look at it, and write down why you think you chose that card if you had to guess.

If you don't have any cards, get a magazine, open any page, skim through, pick a headline or image that catches your eye, and write down why you feel you chose it.

After you've finished writing your opinion, go in by reciting the Key. Take a moment to feel the shift and ask out loud: "Am I in?"

Did you hear it, see it, feel it, or all of the above?

If "yes," then congratulations! You can skip down to the ^ symbol to do the exercise.

If you did not hear it or see it clearly, ask: "Am I in?"

Wait, give it a moment. Ask again. If nothing, ask: "Why can't I see, hear, or feel you?"

If blank, ask: "What's behind the blankness?" "Give me more."

Be patient, feel, and ask: Do I need to repeat the Magic Key?

If you feel different, ask: What am I feeling? And so on....

^ **Once you are in**, ask about your card or the media clip you picked:

> · Why did I pick this card? (Get your pen moving, ask again, or write out the question. Then write down everything you hear, see, feel, or know at that moment.)

Feel free to go deeper:

> · What's the message/benefit for me?

> · Is there a connection to another lifetime? If so, what is it? (Other lifetimes may start with one element or scene, so identify it and ask for more.)

> · Anything else?

Then close out by saying, "Thank you. Thank you. Thank you."

Feel the shift.

Now, compare your answers. Did you get anything new? What are the differences?

Chapter 18

Access to Everyone

Exercise 2

You can explore, consult, and skills build from the greats. There is no limit. Here's an introduction.

Out of the records, write down the first name that pops in:

1. Pick a Master Teacher or Saint:

2. Pick a "dead" person, known to you or famous:

3. Pick a famous living person:

Write out any reasons you may have for choosing these people.

1. Master Teacher or Saint:

2. "Dead" person:

3. Famous living person:

Now go in and ask if you're in. As long as you followed the directions, you are in, so play along. Ask each of the following questions to each person you chose so you can have a conversation. (If you're not getting anything, get your pen moving.)

1. Is _____ (Master or Saint) available to speak?

    · Hello. What is or was your gift to the world?

    · What is your message to me?

    · What's the benefit of this exchange for me?

    · From your perspective, was your work effective? Are you satisfied?

· Do you miss being here?

· Is there anything else you want to tell me?

· [Finish the interview. You may want to continue at a later time.] Thank you for speaking with me. Then move on to the next.

2. Is _____ (the deceased) available to speak?

· Hello. What was your impact on the world?

· What is your message to me?

· What's the benefit of this exchange for me?

· From your perspective, was your work effective? Are you satisfied?

· Do you miss being here?

· Is there anything else you wish to share with me?

[Finish] Thank you for speaking with me. Want to continue at a later time?

And, next.

3. Is _____ (famous living person) available to speak?

· Hello. What is your contribution to the world?

· What is your message for me?

· What's the benefit of this exchange for me?

· From your perspective, is your life's work effective? Are you satisfied?

· Is there anything else for us to talk about now?

[Wrap it up] Thank you for connecting with me. Shall we chat later?"

Close out, "Thank you. Thank you. Thank you."

Compare your answers to the answers from your higher self. Was there a difference?

Is that enough for today? If you stop or take a break before continuing, remember to get grounded. You might have gotten warm due to the energy and shifts that occurred. You might be hungry. You will sleep very well tonight!

Chapter 19

Access to Groups

Exercise 3

You have access to all—everything, not just singular energies. You can connect and communicate with multi-energy systems like groups, businesses, causes, gatherings, and so on. You can participate with intentions if you do not have any questions. You can also define an aspect of a group you wish to explore, such as horse riders' animal welfare stewardship. I would call it the animal welfare room in the library of horse riders to play with the library metaphor. You're about to get a taste of all this.

Remember to keep it light so you can practice. Without your higher self:

1. Pick a non-profit organization:

2. Choose a local community issue or concern:

3. Select a worldwide issue or topic:

Write out any reasons you may have for picking them:

1. Organization:

2. Local issue:

3. World issue:

The Akashic Records is often referred to as a library. When exploring groups, you can play with the library metaphor and experience rooms in the library like the Hogwarts Room of Requirement or imagine an inter-dimensional portal so that the Sierra Club room, for example, can look like the garden of Eden filled with plants, flowers, and wildlife.

Now, go in and ask if you're in. Play with the library metaphor, explore, and answer or ask each of the following questions:

1. Take me to the room of _____ (organization).

    · What do you feel? Hear? See? Are you in a physical room?

    · Why did I choose this _____ (room/organization)?

    · What is your message to me?

    · What other information do you wish to tell me about this room?

    · One intention I have for this organization is _____. Please comment.

    · Thank you. Is there more for me to explore later?

    Then move on to the next.

2. Take me to the room of _____ (local issue).

    · What do you feel? Hear? See? Are you in a physical room?

· Why did I pick this _____
(room/issue)?

· What is the message for me here?

· What other information do you want to tell me
about this room?

· An intention I have for this local issues is
_____. Please comment.

· Thank you. Is there more here for me to discover later?

Next.

3. Take me to the room of _____
   (world issue)?

   · What do you feel? Hear? See? Are you in a
   physical room?

   · Why did I select this _____
   (room/issue)?

   · What is one message for me?

   · What else is there for me to know about this

room?

· One intention I have for this world issue is
_____. Please comment.

· Thank you. Is there more for me to discover about this room at a later time?

Compare their answers to your answers. How do they differ? Speak to the Records about the nuances and the process.

Is this enough for today?

If no, play and explore some more. If yes, close out, "Thank you. Thank you. Thank you." Get grounded. How do you feel?

Chapter 20

Exploring
Exercises

Bonus Exploration

The following are questions you can go in and ask. Explore any information within the text that you have already read in this book that may be useful, spark your curiosity further, or possibly challenge you somehow. Remember that these questions are the first step into an unfolding dialog for your expansion and pathway to dissolving limiting beliefs. Refer to the Protocol steps if necessary.

* Intention: Get Grounded

- How do I ground?

- Is it a priority for me to get grounded before my higher self consults?

- Which grounding techniques work best for me?

- Does wearing black socks keep me grounded?

- Help me create a grounding trigger.

* Clarity

- My perception/opinion about _____ is _____. Please comment and shed some light on this topic.

* Deeper understanding

- Is _____ accurate?

- Describe _____ in another way?

- Why does _____ make me uncomfortable?

- What is important about _____ for me?

· Is this _____ for me?

* To feel connected

· How do I nurture myself today?

· How do I surrender more?

· How do I connect to my glorious wonder, wellness, and wisdom?

* Expand awareness

· Is there something hidden about _____?

· What am I not seeing here?

· Help me expand my awareness regarding _____?

* Use archetypes/roles in positive ways

· How is my Saboteur playing out?

· What role does my **Prostitute** play?

· What triggered my **Victim**?

· How can I work with my archetypes?

Archetype Glossary

- Prostitute: pertaining to integrity – what part of ourselves do we compromise and for what? Everyone has this archetype.
- Victim: Caroline Myss describes: *"Don't be misled by the label "victim." In its healthy state, the victim provides us a quality of perception and strength that protects us against being victimized by others. It alerts us to become more conscious in situations that are conducive to our being taken advantage of. However, we need to develop clarity of insight, which means learning the nature and intensity of the victim. In its underdeveloped state, victim consciousness tells us continually that we are always taken advantage of in situations, and it is never our fault. The victim's purpose is to lead us in and out of these situations until we have had enough and stand up for ourselves. We are not meant to be victimized in life; rather, we are meant to learn how to handle the challenges of our lives and to outrun our fears so that we can truly understand the meaning of strength."*

* Harmony

- Where is my blind spot regarding _____?

- What role is denial playing in this situation?

- How do I harmonize with my gloriousness?

- What are the steps to appreciating and celebrating each glorious day?

* Unconditional love

- What is unconditional love?

- How can I express unconditional love?

- Is _____ person with me for a reason, a season, or extended play? Tell me more.

* Settle negative feelings

Pick something that triggers you. A suggestion can be poverty or pain: _____

- Comment on _____?

- What is the original cause of _____?

- Is _____ neutral?

- Are you sure?

- Why does it not feel neutral?

- What causes _____ in me?

- How do I release it?

* Glorious Living

- Is there anything in my way of glorious living? If so, what?

- What are some steps for me to live more gloriously?

- How do I express my glory?

- How do I express my glory more?

- How do I express my most glorious potential?

- In which ways do I deny my gloriousness? Why do I do so?

- How do I deny my wonder, wellness, and wisdom?

· Does everything happen for my benefit?

* Wonder

· How do I tap into more wonder?

· How is my spirit expressed as wonder?

· How can my spirit express itself as wonder?

· What other wonder is possible for me?

* Wellness

· How do I tap into wellness?

· How can my body express greater wellness?

· What is my wellness potential?

· What self-care is a priority for me now?

* Wisdom

· How do I best express my wisdom?

· Where is my blind spot regarding _____?

- How does my perception of the future limit me?

- What is my wisdom potential?

- What question am I not asking that is a priority for me to ask at this time?

* Get out of my own way

- When consulting, how do I tell the difference between me (my personality) and my higher self (Akashic Records)?

- What assumptions am I making regarding _____?

- How is _____ assumption affecting me?

- How do I integrate my _____ (limitation such as perfectionism) and my infiniteness?

- How do I connect to my infinite nature?

- How can I connect to my infinite nature?

- What came first, the chicken or the egg?

* Empowerment

- Why do struggle and suffering create expansion?

- Please explain the manifestation principle and order of Be, Do, Have?

- What do I need to know about awakening my wizard within?

- Why am I learning this?

- Is all this real?

Exit by saying, "Thank you. Thank you. Thank you" out loud. Get grounded.

Chapter 21

Awakened Wizards

New Grad Group

Now that you have the Key, gone in, and explored the Akashic Records with your higher self, you can join our private Awakened Wizards Facebook Group for graduates only, and be a part of our Wizarding community. You can ask questions, get support, and meet fellow Wizards.

The website address is facebook.com/groups/AwakenedWizards and the password to join is *Wombat*.

Chapter 22

Sample Consultation

Limiting Beliefs

We can reprogram old patterning or limiting beliefs such as "there is not enough time in the day." I included this exchange because viewing time as limited is one of my wounds and one many of us share.

MB = Macarena Luz Bianchi
HS = Higher Self Consulting

I went in with the Key.

MB: What is the root cause of this belief?

HS: Cultural

MB: What do I need to know to release it?

HS: It is not the truth and it is not useful. Time is neutral. It is your perception of time that gives it a positive or negative charge.

MB: Anything else?

HS: Yes, you have another limiting belief affecting you: the idea that work creates self-worth. As you know, you overwork because part of you doesn't remember you are infinitely and unconditionally worthy despite what you do or don't do.

MB: Is that also cultural?

HS: The root cause is cultural and reinforced in many lifetimes.

MB: Are any details about those lifetimes necessary for me to know?

HS: No

MB: Okay, culture as explained in the novel Ishmael by Daniel Quinn?

HS: Yes, reading it brought these concepts into focus so you could make a choice.

MB: Is it that simple? All I have to do is accept there is plenty of time?

HS: Yes, it is always simple.

MB: So how is it shifting right now?

HS: The energy exchange of this message is shifting it. The integration happens as you continue to choose moment by moment. Remember this law: when the self is taken care of first, everything else is taken care of.

MB: Okay, but is there evidence to prove that in the physical world?

HS: Yes, you will find what you seek. Talk to people who are successful internally (at peace, in joy, expressive) and externally (have what they require) and ask them about their journey. Your next question would be, how do I take care of myself?

MB: Okay, how?

HS: The physical, emotional, and spiritual expression, nurturing, and nourishment you require will vary from day to day. You can ask what your priorities are for expression, nurturing, and nourishment.

MB: What about today?

HS: Integrate your new belief "I have plenty of time to gloriously take care of myself, create (work), and play" by breathing and feeling what that feels like.

MB: I feel free and expansive... energy is flowing through me, I feel love. I feel loved.

HS: Now you can access this feeling every time you think or say, "I have plenty of time to gloriously take care of myself, create (work), and play.

MB: Thank you, you guys rock!

HS: (laughter) It's our job. Thanks for letting us.

MB: Thank you. Thank you. Thank you.

Feeling great, I soak it in and then get grounded by walking barefoot.

Your Turn

Do you relate to anything in the Sample Consultation? If so, you can go in, state your perspective, and have a consultation about it.

Farewell

Dear Enchanting Wizard,

Congratulations on exploring, discovering, and claiming who you are! Love, divinity, knowledge, and power are you, all of you. I admire your courage to look within and love that you've awakened the Wizard and accessed your innate divinity, unlimited knowledge, and infinite power! You've integrated the divinity within, the divinity without, and the divinity throughout. How does it feel to be aware? How does it feel to be free? How will you express it? Use it well, express your glory, and share your joy!

With infinite opportunities come infinite questions. Feel free to ask anything that comes to you. The Wizard within will work with you. Keep an open heart, mind, and feel Love.

Please stay in touch via our Awakened Wizards Facebook Group. If you mention this work outside our group, you can use the hashtag #awakenthewizardwithin, and you can invite people to the Awaken the Wizard Within Facebook Group.

I'd love to hear your feedback about this book, testimonials, and questions, which I will do my best to answer. This work grows via your word of mouth, so I appreciate you for sharing it with those who are ready and reviewing it on Amazon.

As far as continuing this course of study, check out my online courses Level 1 Awaken the Wizard Within like the Biofeedback & Muscle Testing and the other Level 2 like More Magic and Enchanting Practice with 40 days of exercises in different topics designed to get you comfortable with this precious magic and fully integrate the Wizard. These are also available in books.

Enjoy the freedom and fun of our metaphysical reality. As a Wizard, may you create an enchanting and luminous life filled with glorious wonder, wellness, and wisdom!

With love and gratitude,
Macarena Luz Bianchi
Your Virtual Fairy Godmother

Troubleshooting

"Wonder is the beginning of wisdom." ~ Lao Tzu

Having troubles? Not to worry; you are not cursed. Everything you require is within this text.

Let's Review

It is critical to follow all the directions precisely when reciting the Key. The Key, if said correctly, accesses the Wizard. What may take some people practice is the ability to clear the mind, the patience to receive, recognizing you're in, and knowing the difference between their thoughts and emotions and their higher self. I suffered from all of these and eventually realized I was in all along.

Let's start with some mechanics:

1. Have you read and signed the Wizarding Agreement? It serves as your contract with pure conscious-

137

ness to step into this work consciously. The act of signing energizes your intent.

2. Have you read all the text? It infuses you with a translator that instantly deciphers the energetic information received from your higher self so that you may use it consciously while awake.

3. Have you had alcohol or recreational drugs within the last 24 hours of going in? This will interfere with the transmission.

4. Are your feet flat on the ground without your arms, legs, or feet crossed? Crossing limbs interrupts your energy circuit.

5. How did you prepare for the session? Did you have a clear mind and an open heart?

6. When you recite the Key, do you say it twice: the first time out loud and the second time in silence in your mind to yourself while replacing "my" with your legal first and last name in the possessive tense? For example, I say to myself (in silence) the second time, "... of Macarena Bianchi's soul..."

7. While saying the Key and immediately right after, what did you feel? Any shift? When you asked, *am I in*, did you feel, hear, see, or know anything? Did you

rewrite the questions to get your hand moving without editing? Did you write down everything that came to you? If you felt, heard, or saw nothing, did you ask for the communication to be bigger or louder? The idea is to ask and feel, see, hear the response.

8. If you feel any difference after saying the Key, you are in. So do all the exercises even if you do not feel/think you are communicating. Pretend if you have to, at the beginning. Eventually, you will know it is not only your personality coming through. Even today, I constantly double-check whether I'm in and always ask for confirmation about where the information is coming from. Am I in? Are you sure? Is that coming from you or me? Is this accurate? Is my interpretation correct?

9. Review the course material again. Re-read this book. Some may benefit from the Awaken the Wizard Within 1001 online course, which includes everything in this book with videos.

10. If you still need extra help, schedule a private session.

Resources & References

Macarena Luz Bianchi macarenaluzb.com for courses, sessions, and more.

Spark Social Press sparksocialpress.com

Subscribe to the email list for this book spark.fyi/1001

Awaken the Wizard Within Facebook Group facebook.com/groups/AwakenTheWizardWithin

Awakened Wizards Facebook Group facebook.com/groups/AwakenedWizards

#awakenthewizardwithin

In Order Listed

You can find a list of clickable links at spark.fyi/1001 or macarenaluzbianchi.com/books/1001.

Abraham Hicks on YouTube youtube.com/results?search_query=abraham+hicks

Conversations with God amzn.to/2qfdJs0

Amazing Secrets of the Masters of the Far East amzn.to/2pH1m82

Edgar Cayce on the Akashic Records amzn.to/2pGR1ZS

Sacred Contracts amzn.to/2oQTeNE

Harry Potter and the Sorcerer's Stone amzn.to/31JjBLo

Natural Healing Book amzn.to/2pdy67F

Yolanda Valdez yolandavaldes.com

Janet Galipo 2behealthyinc.com

Akashic Record Consultants International arc-akashicrecords.org

Indigo Children amzn.to/2qogxiV

Kryon amzn.to/2pudp86

Diana Cooper amzn.to/2pdWDcx

The Hidden Messages in Water amzn.to/2pqBMBh

What the Bleep do We Know? amzn.to/2pqp31r

You Can Heal Your Life amzn.to/2oGxAQJ

The Isaiah Effect amzn.to/3kyFmUQ

Abraham-Hicks amzn.to/2qnYERe

Shaun of the Dead amzn.to/2JrbQU5

The Present amzn.to/2pdHkRp

The Four Agreements amzn.to/2HBBfKn

Deepak Chopra amzn.to/2ADSnaa

Mastery of Love amzn.to/3q77QZY

One Minute for Yourself: A Simple Strategy for a Better Life amzn.to/2KfkJ3F

The Five Tibetans amzn.to/39ZMYyh

Getting the Love You Want amzn.to/37VehXF

Love and Awakening: Discovering the Sacred Path of Intimate Relationship amzn.to/2iQ1Qmn

Secrets of the Millionaire Mind: Mastering the Inner Game of Wealth amzn.to/2hsORus

Master Key System amzn.to/2Y4QMWA

Who Moved My Chesse? amzn.to/36heKny

Universal Compassion: Transforming Your Life through Love and Compassion amzn.to/2ytHXZ9

Sacred Contracts amzn.to/2zQQ8TJ

The Matrix amzn.to/2ADD5lt

The Matrix Reloaded amzn.to/2ADD5lt

Hogwarts Room of Requirement pottermore.com/features/everything-you-need-to-know-about-the-room-of-requirement

Carolyn Myss amzn.to/3nfinjV

About the Author

Macarena Luz Bianchi is a personal development coach and holistic practitioner. She's kindly known as a Fairy Godmother to her clients. Her lighthearted empowerment approach helps people tap into their glory through wonder, wellness, and wisdom.

She created the Awaken the Wizard Within material and courses to teach simple yet powerful metaphysical tools. She has found problems, imbalances, and dissatisfaction with life arise when people ignore their energetic side. Her nondenominational sensibility stems from growing up atheist in Catholic cultures, where she noticed that individuals who displaced responsibility on external factors led to their disempowerment.

She specializes in self-esteem building. She can see how individuals program themselves for disempowerment because she's done her own work and helped her clients build consistent and sustainable confidence. The Hot Project is her makeover-system that gets builds an individual's confidence foundation so their self-esteem can blossom from the inside out.

She writes fiction and non-fiction for adults and children.

Originally from Santiago, Chile, she lives in Miami, Florida, and online at macarenaluzb.com, where you can sign up for her newsletter, get some useful freebies and explore her Lighthearted Empowerment Academy.

Macarena Luz Bianchi's
LIGHTHEARTED EMPOWERMENT ACADEMY

MEMBERSHIP CLUBS
The Hot Project Club is a monthly Self-Esteem Makeover from the Inside Out

ONLINE COURSES
Awaken the Wizard Within | Level I

- 101 Biofeedback & Muscle Testing for Muggles

- 102 Light's Counterpart to Negativity - Energy Management & Alignment

- 103 Glorious Living with Wonder, Wellness & Wisdom - Energy Management

Awaken the Wizard Within | Level II

- 1001 Higher Self Consulting & Akashic Records Reading

- 1002 More Magic for Awakened Wizards

- 1003 Enchanting Practice for Awakened Wizards

Awaken the Wizard Within | Level III

- 2001 Higher Self Consulting & Reading the Akashic Records for Others

- 3001 Teaching Higher Self Consulting

BOOKS
Awaken the Wizard Within Series Level I to IV

- Level I: *Muscle Testing & Biofeedback for Muggles: Awaken the Wizard Within 101*
- Level II: *More Magic for Awakened Wizards: Awaken the Wizard Within 1002*
- Level II: *Enchanting Practice for Awakened Wizards: Awaken the Wizard Within 1003 Workbook*

Gratitude Is Series

- *Gratitude Is: The Poem and Lighthearted Empowerment Keys to Feeling Grateful*
- *Gratitude Is: A Lighthearted Empowerment Poem* Gift Book
- *Gratitude Is: Poem & Coloring Book*
- *The Grateful Giraffes: What is Gratitude?* Children's Book

The Hot Project Series

- *Yes, You're Hot! The Step-by-Step Guide to Sizzling Self-Esteem Inside and Out*

Your Fairy Godmother's Guide to Life Series

RaveAlone! A Coming of Age Story: The Screenplay & Production Notes